AVATI

Discovering Arctic Ecology

Acknowledgements

Special thanks to the following researchers, experts, and authors for their valued input in reviewing the text: Steve Ferguson, Mark Mallory, Carolyn Mallory, Shannon Badzinski, and Justin Buller.

Published by Inhabit Media Inc. • www.inhabitmedia.com
Inhabit Media Inc. (Iqaluit), P.O. Box 11125, Iqaluit, Nunavut, X0A 1H0 • (Toronto), 301-191 Eglinton Ave. E. Toronto, Ontario, M4P 1K1

Design and layout copyright © 2012, 2021 Inhabit Media Inc. • Text copyright © 2012, 2021 by Mia Pelletier • Illustrations copyright © 2012, 2021 by Sara Otterstätter • Map illustration copyright © 2012 by John Lightfoot

We acknowledge the support of the Canada Council for the Arts for our publishing program.

This project has been made possible in part by the Government of Canada.

Printed in Canada

Library and Archives Canada Cataloguing in Publication

Title: Avati : discovering Arctic ecology / by Mia Pelletier ; illustrated by Sara Otterstätter.
Other titles: Discovering Arctic ecology
Names: Pelletier, Mia, author. | Otterstätter, Sara, 1978- illustrator.
Description: Previously published: Iqaluit, Nunavut ; Toronto, Ontario : Inhabit Media Inc., ©2012.
Identifiers: Canadiana 20210104872 | ISBN 9781772272949 (softcover)
Subjects: LCSH: Ecology—Arctic regions—Juvenile literature.
Classification: LCC QH84.1 .P44 2021 | DDC j577.0911/3—dc23

AVATI
Discovering Arctic Ecology

By Mia Pelletier

Illustrated by
Sara Otterstätter

INHABIT
MEDIA

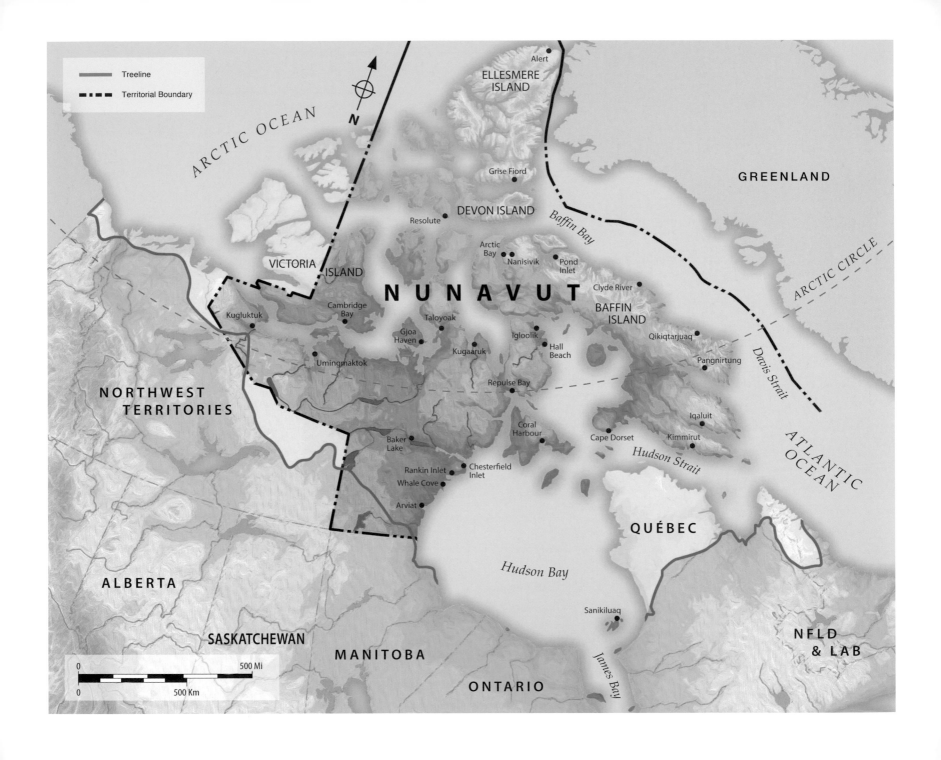

Legend
— Treeline
—··— Territorial Boundary

ARCTIC OCEAN

N

ELLESMERE ISLAND

Alert

GREENLAND

Grise Fiord

DEVON ISLAND

Resolute

Baffin Bay

Arctic Bay

VICTORIA ISLAND

NUNAVUT

Nanisivik

Pond Inlet

Clyde River

BAFFIN ISLAND

ARCTIC CIRCLE

Kugluktuk

Cambridge Bay

Taloyoak

Gjoa Haven

Kugaaruk

Igloolik

Hall Beach

Qikiqtarjuaq

Pangnirtung

Davis Strait

Umingmaktok

Repulse Bay

NORTHWEST TERRITORIES

Iqaluit

Coral Harbour

Cape Dorset

Kimmirut

Baker Lake

Rankin Inlet

Chesterfield Inlet

Whale Cove

Arviat

Hudson Strait

ATLANTIC OCEAN

QUÉBEC

ALBERTA

Hudson Bay

NFLD & LAB

SASKATCHEWAN

Sanikiluaq

MANITOBA

James Bay

ONTARIO

0   500 Mi
0   500 Km

On many maps, the Arctic appears as a vast field of white. Yet, it is a land that changes endlessly as you travel across it—from frozen ocean, icy blue glaciers, and towering mountains to green river valleys, boggy wetlands, and rolling hills. The boundaries of this region are defined in many ways. Some describe the Arctic as the part of the world that lies within the Arctic Circle. This imaginary line circles the globe at the top of the world to mark the place where the sun does not fully rise or set for at least one day of the year. Trace your finger along this line, and you will pass through the northern parts of several countries around the world, including the Yukon, the Northwest Territories, and Nunavut in northern Canada.

The Arctic can also be described as the part of the world that lies above the "treeline." As you travel north, trees become smaller and smaller, then vanish entirely as it becomes too difficult for trees to grow. The treeline rises and falls as it winds across the map of northern Canada, and onwards around the globe.

Yet for the Arctic peoples that have lived in this region for thousands of years, the Arctic is simply home. *Avati* means "environment" in Inuktitut, the Inuit language. While many of the plants and animals found in this book can be found in other parts of the Arctic, we'll explore the landscapes of Nunavut, the part of the Arctic whose name means "our land."

The name "Arctic" comes from the Greek word for bear, *arktos*. It describes the constellations of stars that you can see in the northern night sky. See their shapes in the starry sky? These are *Ursa Major* and *Ursa Minor*, the Great Bear and the Little Bear. These stars shine over the Arctic, the icy wilderness of treeless *tundra* and frozen ocean that lies at the top of the world.

From a distance, this bare, windswept landscape appears empty. Covered by ice and snow for much of the year, the Arctic winter is long, cold, and dark. Yet spring and summer bring an explosion of life. As the ice retreats from the land and sea, great flocks of birds arrive from the south, the ocean blooms with life, and tundra plants reach for the sun with new leaves, shoots, and berries.

Let's explore the Arctic through the seasons. We'll see that this landscape is not empty at all, but contains many unique *habitats*, and plants and animals found nowhere else on Earth. From the millions of tiny insects to the great polar bear, each *species* is an important part of the Arctic *web of life*, and all species depend on one another in the struggle to survive.

Here at the *floe edge*, *landfast ice* meets open ocean and mist rises in the chilly air. The spring sun has just risen high enough to shine through the seawater. It glows on the underside of the sea ice, illuminating an underwater garden of tiny algae. These *ice algae* use energy from the sun to grow so thick that they turn the ice a golden brown. Small, shrimp-like animals called *amphipods* graze on this rich food. As amphipods eat the ice algae, Arctic cod use their jutting lower jaws to scoop up the amphipods from this hanging garden.

Splash! *Gulp*! Arctic cod are an important food for many marine mammals, including ringed seals. Seabirds that have travelled from near and far to the Arctic to nest are also hungry for fish. Thick-billed murres gather in great numbers at the floe edge. Here they dive for the fish they need to build up energy to lay and *incubate* their eggs. An Inuit hunter has also come to the floe edge to hunt. He listens for the wet breath of narwhals as they glide through the water with their long ivory tusks.

The sheer cliffs of the Arctic island coasts offer many nesting places for seabirds. After filling their bellies with fish, thick-billed murres head for the sea cliffs to lay their eggs. "*Aoorrr, aoorr!*" Murres join the crowded colony, one by one, until the sound of their calls is a continuous roar. Each murre finds its place on a narrow rock ledge to lay its one beautiful, speckled turquoise egg. Pointed on one end and round on the other, their eggs are specially shaped to roll in a circle so they don't fall off the cliff. Hungry glaucous gulls patrol the cliffs like sentries on a castle wall, watching for eggs to steal and eat. An Arctic fox sniffs the beach below, searching for lost eggs. Murre droppings provide rich fertilizer for the growth of jewel *lichen*, which paints the rocks beneath the nest cliffs a brilliant orange.

In early summer, the ocean below the cliffs may still be frozen, and murres must fly out across the sea ice to dive for food in a *polynya*. Here, wind and currents keep a patch of ocean free of ice, and *upwelling* brings nutrients up from the ocean floor. Polynyas are a refuge in the ice for many marine animals throughout the winter, and now they fill with life. Tiny, floating plants called *phytoplankton* feed small, drifting animals called *zooplankton*. In turn, zooplankton provide food for fish, seabirds, and larger animals, like whales. The water teems with life as murres join the northern fulmars and black-legged kittiwakes that have also come to feast.

Murres are just one of many species that use the Arctic as a nursery. From all over the world, birds travel to the Arctic in the millions to raise their young. The most incredible journey is that of the Arctic tern, which travels 70,000 kilometres round trip from Antarctica to nest in the Arctic every year. This is the longest *migration* of any bird on Earth.

"*Kek-kek-kek*!" Arctic terns nest on the ground in noisy colonies, *plunge-diving* for *marine invertebrates* and fish. Fierce defenders of their eggs, terns will aggressively attack any *predator* that enters the colony. To benefit from this protection, a female red phalarope has laid her speckled eggs close by. She spins in circles on a nearby pond, making a whirlpool that traps *aquatic* bugs, which she plucks from the water and eats. Enjoying one last meal, she leaves her mate behind to incubate her eggs. His less colourful feathers blend in so perfectly with the tundra that he cannot be seen.

"*Feee-leerrr*!" The dark shadow of a parasitic jaeger flies over the colony. Often feeding on food stolen from other birds, this stealthy pirate swoops quickly, knocking a fish from the bill of a flying tern and catching it in the air before it falls. Lost fish and bird droppings nourish the soil beneath the colony, where a thick mat of green moss grows.

"A h-WOO-oo!" Just over the hill, the ghostly calls of a *raft* of common eiders drift in from the ocean where they've been diving for mussels. Having stored up lots of fat, female eiders build their nests upon the ground. Lining their nests with soft, grey down plucked from their breasts, eiders keep their eggs snug and warm beneath them. Eiderdown is so warm that it is collected by Inuit from nests across the tundra. To spot nesting eiders, you must look carefully. The eiders' mottled brown feathers camouflage them so well that they seem to disappear. Even as a light snow falls and dusts their wings, the hens will not leave their nests, nor will they eat for the twenty-five days it takes for their eggs to hatch. As they wait, the hens survive on fat stores in their bodies.

This year there are many lemmings on the tundra, and the eider colony is protected from some predators by the pair of snowy owls nesting nearby. As lemmings line their underground nests with soft feathers and grasses to raise their many *litters*, the male owl hunts for lemmings to feed his mate and chases away the Arctic foxes that come near. Arctic foxes love to hunt lemmings, but they are also excellent egg thieves. Foxes bury the eggs they steal in *caches* underground. In the dark and hungry days of winter, foxes return to these spots to dig up their secret stashes.

As the summer sun climbs higher, the surface of the tundra soil begins to warm. But not far beneath the surface lies the *permafrost*, a layer of frozen earth that never thaws. Permafrost prevents water from soaking deep into the ground, so snowmelt pools in every hollow on the tundra. Mosquito eggs, laid the year before, hatch into *larvae* in puddles, ponds, and lakes. The tiny larvae feed on plankton and grow quickly.

Water and mud are home to many insects that are important foods for birds, especially the larvae of midges and crane flies. From all over the world, millions of *shorebirds* have flocked to the Arctic to feast on insects and raise their young. They lay their eggs on bare ground, or in a simple nest lined with lichen, moss, or grass. Their camouflaged feathers and *cryptic* eggs make shorebirds and their nests very difficult to see. Can you see them? *"Prreep! Prreep!"* A least sandpiper picks his way along the soggy shore, probing the mud for tasty bugs. *Splash*! A long-tailed duck dives to capture aquatic insects, using his wings to propel him deep into the pond.

BzzzzZZZZZZ. The quiet of the tundra is broken as mosquito larvae grow into adults and the air fills with the hum of buzzing biters. While mosquitoes provide food for many birds, female mosquitoes can follow an animal's breath in the air to reach their own warm meal. The barren ground caribou that graze on the first green shoots of summer are nearly driven mad by the hungry swarms. They walk into the wind and rest on the last few patches of snow to try to avoid the mosquitoes' bites.

In the far North, the Peary caribou have exchanged their thick, white winter coats for short, dark summer coats. Their large, crescent-shaped hooves make excellent paddles, which propel them easily across rivers and between islands as they roam in search of nutritious plants. While Peary caribou eat many kinds of grasses, *sedges*, lichen, and mushrooms, their favourite plant, the purple saxifrage, now fills the landscape with colour. Their muzzles are stained purple from grazing as they build up fat reserves for the coming winter.

The Peary caribou's keen sense of smell helps them find food, but they have not sensed the pair of Arctic wolves that has been silently tracking the herd. The wolves have watched patiently with their golden eyes, looking for caribou that are young, old, or weak. The herd spots the wolves and makes a dash for higher ground. Caribou can often outrun wolves, but one young calf is not fast enough to keep up. The long-legged wolves bound across the tundra, closing in. In the distance, a wolverine has also been following the herd. When the wolves have filled their bellies with meat, the wolverine will feed on the remains of the carcass left behind.

Now it is high summer on the tundra and the sun circles the sky but never sets. Flower buds, which have waited all winter beneath the snow, unfold in the light. To escape strong winds, many plants grow tight to the ground in dense cushions. Dark leaves and stems absorb the sun's heat, and fine hairs trap insulating air. Some plants, like Arctic poppies, have flowers that turn to follow the sun as it moves across the sky. These flowers offer a warm shelter for insects that come to sunbathe inside them.

Insects are an essential part of Arctic *ecosystems*, as they break down plant and animal material and *pollinate* flowers. They, too, have many ways of keeping warm during the cool Arctic summer. Dark, hairy bodies absorb heat from the sun and trap a warm layer of air. Dark butterflies use their wings to collect the sun's warmth, while white butterflies may use their wings like mirrors to reflect sunrays onto their bodies. Bumblebees shiver their flight muscles to keep warm.

The tundra teems with insect life. The luminous wings of Arctic blue butterflies shine as they dine on flower nectar. Aphids climb through the saxifrage, feeding on leaf juice. A carrion beetle, with its keen sense of smell, searches the air for the scent of an animal carcass. Wolf spiders hunt for insects on the ground, nearly invisible in their camouflage coats, while sheet web spiders spin webs into silky balloons and float away on the wind.

The plants of the summer tundra provide a lush feast for Arctic *herbivores*, which spread seeds and nourish plants with their droppings. All summer, muskoxen have roamed the tundra feeding on willows, grasses, and herbs, and they have built up a thick layer of fat for the coming winter. Crowned with large, curved horns and wearing a thick woolly coat, Inuit call muskoxen "*umingmak,*" meaning "the bearded one." Their long, shaggy hair snags on plants and is stolen underground by lemmings to line the nests of their last summer litters. *Smash! Clang!* The air fills with the crash of the muskoxen's hefty horns as bulls challenge each other for the right to mate with females. Beneath their fleecy coats, they have already grown a thick layer of *qiviut* wool in preparation for the coming cold. Grown every autumn and shed each spring, this soft, warm wool will be gathered by Inuit from across the tundra in the coming seasons.

Snow geese and tundra swans have also raised their young on Arctic plants. Snow geese graze damp soils for tasty sedges, seeds, and aquatic plants, while tundra swans nibble on plants that grow in shallow water. Young tundra swans, called *cygnets*, can grow up to twenty-eight times their hatch weight during the short Arctic summer. They must be ready to fly by summer's end, when swans leave for more southern waters. Soon, Arctic char will also be on their way. After feeding in the ocean all summer, their brilliant orange and silver *scales* shine as they wind up Arctic rivers to winter in the depths of tundra lakes. Inuit fishermen gather at the river mouths to catch these sparkling fish as they go.

As summer fades, the last of the shorebirds that have raised their young on the tundra fly south along the ocean coasts. The Arctic fills with the sound of beating wings and the cries of geese, ducks, swans, and cranes as huge flocks take to the skies like long arrows pointing south. The low mats of plants that have fed caribou, Arctic hares, and ptarmigans turn a brilliant red. Crowberries, cloudberries, blueberries, and cranberries grow fat and ripe. The last feathery plumes of mountain avens unwind, releasing their seeds into the wind.

Seeds are also spread by Arctic ground squirrels, lemmings, voles, and seed-eating birds. *"Twee-turee-twee-turiwee!"* The musical call of a snow bunting can be heard as he feasts on summer seeds. *"Tek! Tek!"* A northern wheatear forages on the ground for berries and pounces from his perch to catch one last fly. While some Arctic insects survive the winter frozen in the soil, many insects find sheltered spots inside plant clumps or under stones.

Each day, the autumn sun sinks a little lower in the sky. As its warmth leaves the Arctic, only the hardiest animals remain to face the coming cold. Winter comes quickly. First ponds, then lakes and rivers, begin to freeze. In the growing dark, a light snow begins to fall.

In the dark of winter, the shimmering *aurora* winds through the sky like a green river of fire. Although little snow falls, it is endlessly rearranged by the wind. The patterns formed by wind and snow are so numerous that Inuit have given them many names. *Maniilagalaak* is rough snow and ice, while *uqaluraq* is a pointed drift that looks like a tongue.

Many Arctic animals change the colour of their coats to disappear against the snow. The lush, white coats of ermines, Arctic hares, and Arctic foxes allow them to move secretly through the winter landscape in perfect camouflage. Collared lemmings also turn pale white, and grow long snow-scraper claws that help them dig tunnels through the snow. Their tunnels wind like hidden highways as they pass the winter nibbling on Arctic willow bark. But snow won't hide them from the ermines, foxes, or snowy owls that listen for lemmings from above. Special circles of feathers direct the slightest sound of movement to the owl's ears as it hovers over the frozen drifts.

Many Arctic plants are *wintergreen*, with leaves that survive all winter beneath the snow. While some caribou herds migrate south for the winter, other herds wander the frozen tundra, using their wide hooves to paw through snow in search of lichen, herbs, and grasses. Caribou are just one of the many animals with feet that are specially adapted to help them navigate through the icy Arctic winter. Muskoxen also have wide hooves, which make travel over snow much easier. The edges of their hooves are sharp and curved, perfect for breaking through ice and snow to graze. As muskoxen open up little patches of tundra with their hooves, rock ptarmigans use these openings to search for tasty plants.

"*Cr-r-ruck*! *Cr-r-ruck*!" Ravens have thick, bumpy skin on the bottoms of their feet so that only parts of their feet touch the icy ground. Arctic foxes grow fur on the soles of their feet to keep them warm, while Arctic hares have big, padded feet with long, curved claws to help them dig through the snow for Arctic willow twigs. "*Ko-ko krrow krrow krrow*!" Willow ptarmigans survive the winter by feeding on willow buds beneath the snow. Their feathered feet act like snowshoes as they run across the frozen drifts. They dive beneath the snow to stay warm, leaping from the air so that they do not leave tracks for a predator to follow. The largest falcon in the world, the gyrfalcon, hunts for willow ptarmigan. *Swoosh*! Swooping at speeds of up to 200 kilometres per hour, he dives silently toward his *prey*.

As the temperature drops, seawater freezes to Arctic coastlines as landfast ice. Further offshore, it forms into sheets of floating *pack ice* that break apart and flow with ocean currents. Sea ice provides a critical feeding habitat and safe place for many marine animals.

Ice-loving walruses are well adapted to life on the ice. Using pieces of ice as platforms, walruses dive for clams on the ocean floor and use their long ivory tusks to pull themselves up onto the ice to rest. Their thick *blubber* keeps them warm in the chilly water, and their rough flippers provide traction on slippery ice. Diving to the ocean floor and standing on their heads, walruses feel for prey in the bottom *sediments* with their many rows of sensitive whiskers, called *vibrissae*.

Woosh! The walrus blows a strong jet of water from his nose to clear away the sediment and expose a tasty bed of clams. *Slurp*! The walrus uses his powerful mouth to suck clams right out of the shell. As the walrus eats, bits of clam sink down and provide food for the bottom-dwellers living on the ocean floor, and the cycle continues.

Many Arctic animals rely on sea ice. For polar bears and Arctic foxes, sea ice is a hunting ground. For Peary caribou, sea ice is a highway that allows travel from island to island as they graze on plants beneath the snow. For seals, sea ice offers protection from predators and a surface for bearing pups. As sea ice covers Arctic waters, ringed seals are busy with their sharp claws, making and maintaining *breathing holes* in the landfast ice. Female seals also dig out snowdrifts above their breathing holes to make lairs for resting and giving birth.

Crack! *Crack*! Further offshore, whales spend the winter among the pack ice. Bowhead whales break through new ice as it forms in order to breathe. They can break ice that is up to twenty centimetres thick with their massive heads. Their huge *baleen*-lined mouths strain tiny animals, like *copepods* and *krill*, from the water as they glide through the icy sea. Narwhals are also at home beneath the floating pack ice. Small cracks and *leads* provide access to squid, Greenland halibut, Arctic cod, and shrimp, while deep areas with heavy pack ice provide good protection from predators. Beluga whales swim among the pack ice, breaking breathing holes in the ice with their backs and using their flexible lips to suck Arctic cod out of cracks in the sea ice. Sometimes belugas can get trapped in the pack ice, where they become easy prey for roaming bears.

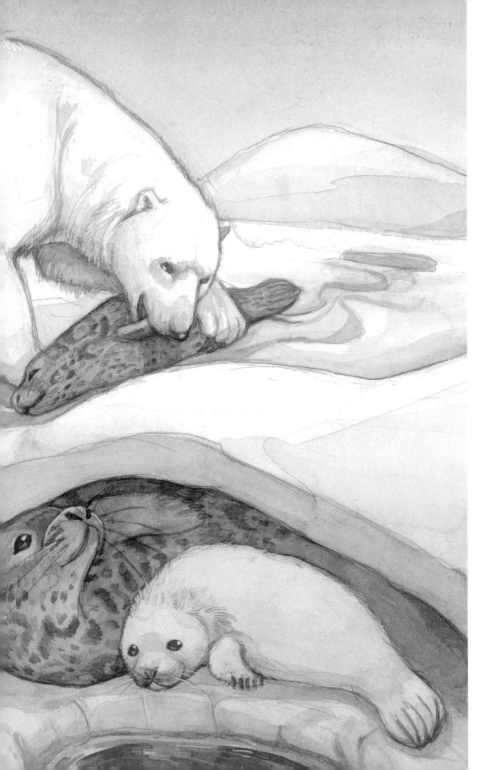

Winter is a time of rich feasting for polar bears. They must use this season to build up thick fat reserves for the coming summer when the sea ice will retreat. Camouflaged in their warm, white coats, polar bears are made for life on the sea ice and rely on this habitat to reach their prey. Skilled hunters with powerful jaws and sharp claws, polar bears hunt bearded, harp, and hooded seals, but prefer eating ringed seal blubber. The bears' wide, partially webbed feet make them excellent swimmers, and they cross easily through open leads as they travel over the ice.

All winter, polar bears have hunted seals at the floe edge, at leads, or by waiting patiently at breathing holes. Inuit hunters call these breathing holes *agluit*, and they, too, have waited by these openings for seals. Now spring is coming, and seal pups, in their snowy white coats, are being born in *birthing lairs* across the sea ice. With their keen sense of smell, polar bears can sniff out young seals across long distances and through thick snow.

Arctic foxes have also roamed the sea ice searching for food. *Sniff*! *Sniff*! Foxes follow their noses to locate seal pups and *carrion*, like dead whales or leftovers from polar bear kills. "*Kree-arr*! *Kree-arr*!" A lone ivory gull soars like a ghost over the frozen sea. This rare white gull also trails polar bears to *scavenge* what they leave behind. Her pale feathers glow in the rising spring sun.

As the sun returns to the Arctic, the silence of the long, dark winter is shattered by the cries of returning birds. Eiders and long-tailed ducks join murres, gulls, and seals, and the floe edge pulses with a new season of life.

Out on the tundra, the herds of caribou that have wintered in the southern forests arrive to bear their calves. Arctic foxes change their bright, white winter coats for secretive summer browns and return to their dens to give birth to their *kits*. Arctic hares nibble on the first new growth of spring, and tundra ponds fill with nesting loons, ducks, and swans. As the winter tunnels of lemmings melt away, snowy owls hunt on the open tundra, and shorebirds return to build their camouflaged nests. Muskoxen shed their winter coats, and qiviut blows like woolly snow across the tundra.

One by one, the buds of purple saxifrage open in the sun, and the tundra blooms with summer colour. Quietly, then growing louder, the first mosquitoes of the new season appear and the cycle of life in the Arctic begins again.

Glossary

amphipod   Small crustaceans with flattened bodies that live in many different habitats. Amphipods can be found in the open sea, on the ocean floor, on the underside of sea ice, on sandy beaches, and among rocks.

aquatic   Of or relating to water. Plants or animals that grow in or live in water are said to be aquatic.

arktos   A Greek word meaning "bear." The Arctic was named after this word, as you can see the Great Bear and Little Bear star constellations from the northern parts of the world.

aurora   Colourful, glowing lights in the night sky that occur when light particles from the sun collide with gases in Earth's atmosphere. The aurora can be seen at both the North and South Poles. In northern parts of the world, the aurora is often called the "northern lights."

baleen   Long, hair-like structures in the mouths of certain whales that are used for straining tiny animals, like krill, from the seawater for food.

birthing lair   A seal's shelter dug out of a snowdrift on the sea ice for the purpose of giving birth.

blubber   A thick, dense layer of fat beneath the skin of marine mammals, like seals and whales, that helps keep them warm in icy waters. Seal blubber is an important source of food for polar bears, and Inuit use the fat as fuel for the *qulliq* (traditional lamp).

breathing hole	A hole in the sea ice that is kept open by seals so that they can come up for air. Seals use their teeth and claws to keep these holes open during the winter.
cache	A secret stash of food that is hidden from other animals and saved for less plentiful times of the year.
carrion	Dead or decaying animal matter, such as carcasses.
copepod	A tiny crustacean that floats along in ocean currents (a kind of zooplankton). Copepods also live on the ocean floor and in other wet places, like lakes and ponds.
cryptic	Colours, markings, or textures that can camouflage an animal within its habitat.
cygnet	A young swan.
ecology	The study of how living things interact with each other and their environment.
ecosystem	All of the plants and animals that share a particular area, and the physical environment with which they interact.
floe edge	The place where the landfast ice ends and the open sea begins. The floe edge is a busy place, where many animals hunt for food in winter and early spring.
habitat	The natural environment in which a plant or an animal lives and is most likely to be found.

herbivore

Animals that eat only plants. For example, Arctic hares and muskoxen are herbivores.

ice algae

Simple organisms that grow on the underside of, and in the spaces within, sea ice. Ice algae use energy from the sun to grow.

incubate

To keep eggs warm by sitting on them so that they can develop and hatch into chicks.

kits

Young foxes. The young of some other fur-bearing mammals, such as beavers, skunks, and weasels, are also called kits.

krill

Small zooplankton that look like shrimp. Krill gather in huge swarms and eat mostly phytoplankton. They are an important food source for many animals in the Arctic Ocean.

landfast ice

Ice that is solidly frozen and attached to the shore or coastline.

larvae

An early stage in the life cycle of amphibians, insects, fish, and some other animals before they grow and change into adults. Larvae hatch from eggs and spend much of their time feeding. Larvae can look very different from adults; for example, a caterpillar is the larva of a butterfly, and a tadpole is the larva of a frog.

leads

Plural of lead; an open channel of water formed when wind or currents move the sea ice.

lichen

An organism that is part fungus and part algae and grows on the surface of rocks, tree trunks, branches, and bare ground. Lichen is often vibrantly coloured and is an important winter food for caribou.

litter

A number of young mammals born together from the same mother.

marine
invertebrates
Animals living in the ocean that do not have an internal skeleton, but may have hard shells. Some examples of marine invertebrates are clams, shrimp, and sea urchins.

migration
An annual or seasonal journey from one place to another in order to find mates, food, or better habitat.

pack ice
Sea ice that is not frozen to the shore, but is made up of pieces of floating ice pushed together by wind and currents. Pack ice provides a place for many marine animals to rest, mate, gain access to food, and avoid predators.

permafrost
A layer of soil or rock beneath the surface that remains frozen all year, even during the summer months.

phytoplankton Tiny plants that drift on ocean currents and make their own food from sunlight.

plunge-diving A method used by some seabirds for catching ocean prey. Seabirds dive from a height of five to twenty metres, tuck in their wings, and plunge into the water to capture food.

pollinate
The process by which wind or animals carry pollen from one flowering plant to another, allowing fertilization and the growth of seeds.

polynya
An open water area surrounded by sea ice that is kept open by wind and ocean currents. Polynyas are places with lots of food for seabirds, walruses, and whales, and are important oases in the frozen ocean during the winter.

predator
An animal that hunts other animals for food.

prey	An animal that is hunted by another animal for food.
raft	A dense flock of birds floating together on the water.
scales	Many overlapping plates that cover fish. Scales provide protection from injury and increase ease of movement through water.
scavenge	To search for food left behind by other animals, or to look for dead and decaying matter to eat. Animals that do this are called scavengers.
sedge	A grasslike plant that grows on wet ground and has triangular stems. Sedges are an important food for caribou, muskoxen, and snow geese.
sediment	Mineral or organic matter that settles to the bottom of an ocean, a lake, or a river. Sediment provides a habitat for bacteria, marine worms, clams, larvae, and some species of fish.
shorebirds	A group of birds that feed along shorelines, marshes, mudflats, and ocean coasts. Shorebirds come in various shapes and sizes and have different adaptations for wet habitats, such as long legs for wading or bills specially shaped to probe for insects and crustaceans among beach stones, in water, or in wet mud and sand.
species	A group of organisms that can breed with one another and produce fertile young.

tundra   A vast, treeless region found in the northern parts of the world with long, cold winters, frozen soils, and low-growing plants.

upwelling   The process by which wind and currents cause cold water to rise up from the bottom of the ocean, bringing nutrients up to the surface where they can be used by plankton to grow.

Ursa Major   "The Great Bear," a constellation of stars that can be seen all year in northern parts of the world. Part of Ursa Major forms the Big Dipper.

Ursa Minor   "The Little Bear," a constellation of stars that can be seen all year in northern parts of the world. These stars make up The Little Dipper, the constellation's common name.

vibrissae   Plural of vibrissa; sensitive, whisker-like hairs that help many mammals sense their environments and find food. Walruses and seals both have vibrissae.

web of life   The complex network of living things, in which each part depends on another for food.

wintergreen   Plants that keep green leaves all year, even beneath the snow; also called "evergreen."

zooplankton   Tiny animals and the larvae of larger animals that float or swim in ocean currents. Zooplankton are different from phytoplankton in that they cannot make their own food, but feed on other zooplankton and phytoplankton.

Notes on Inuktitut Pronunciation

There are some sounds in Inuktitut that may be unfamiliar to English speakers. The pronunciations below convey those sounds in the following ways:

- A double vowel (e.g., aa, ee) lengthens the vowel sound.
- Capitalized letters denote the emphasis for each word.
- q is a "uvular" sound, a sound that comes from the very back of the throat. This is distinct from the sound for k, which is the same as a typical English "k" sound (known as a "velar" sound).
- ll is a rolled "l" sound.

Terms	Pronuncation	Definition
avati	a-VA-ti	environment
maniilagalaak	ma-Nil-la-ga-LAAK	rough snow and ice
qiviut	qi-VIUT	muskox wool
umingmak	u-MING-mak	muskox
uqaluraq	u-QA-lu-raq	pointed drift of snow that looks like a tongue

For more Inuktitut-language resources, visit inhabitmedia.com/inuitnipingit

Mia Pelletier studied ecology and anthropology and holds an MSc from the Durrell Institute of Conservation and Ecology in the United Kingdom. Drawn to wilderness and shorelines, Mia has lived in faraway places from California to the Magdalen Islands and the Canadian Arctic, and spent six years working on the co-management of Arctic protected areas with Inuit communities on Baffin Island. She is the author of *A Children's Guide to Arctic Birds*, and *A Children's Guide to Arctic Butterflies*, which received a 2020 John Burroughs Riverby Award for exceptional natural history books for children.

Sara Otterstätter studied illustration and graphic design at the University for Applied Studies in Münster, Germany. Since 2007, she has been working as a freelance illustrator for German and international publishing houses illustrating children's non-fiction books, colouring books, and games. When not illustrating, she enjoys spending time in nature.

Author's Note

Poets and explorers have famously said that we will protect and conserve only what we love. Yet to love something, we must first know and understand it. This book is for every child who seeks to know a little of the Arctic. While this wondrous place may seem a world apart, it is one of the most ecologically vulnerable places on our rapidly changing planet. I hope that this small glimpse of its complexity leads to greater curiosity and care.

Iqaluit · Toronto
www.inhabitmedia.com